We are sitting at a stop light. We glance at the car next to us. The people are smiling and laughing. We are envious of their seemingly carefree spirit. We are so distraught – deep into sadness and grief. We ask each other:
"Will we ever be able to laugh so easily again?"

We had lost our sweet **sister Susie** to an inoperable brain tumor. She was a naturally joyful person who was deeply faithful and inspiring to all she met. When she realized that she was terminally ill, she faced death with great bravery. Even though she was leaving a husband and four young children, she accepted God's will – **she truly believed** that **"God's plan was better than hers."** Her acceptance made the journey somewhat more tolerable, **but then she was gone...**

We were left in a fog. *A fog of grief.* We just muddled from one day to the next. Anyone who has gone through the loss of a loved one knows that it is unlike any pain ever experienced.
It is tough.
Grief is unique to each and every individual.
There is no timeline, no gold standard for "getting over it."

We had to get out of the fog and leave it behind. Through much prayer and the grace of God, we were inspired to create a service **in memory of Susie – *Dulaya Memories.***
By expressing our grief in a tangible way, we were able to start healing.

May this "I Have You In My Heart" journal help to express your feelings tangibly and begin to lift the fog of grief. The poem was created from what we believed that Susie would want to say to us from heaven.

Perhaps, it is what all of our loved ones would want to say to us.

In loving memory of:

_____

I am with you always, even unto the end of the world. (Matthew 28:20)

Be still and know that I am God. (Psalm 46:10)

... my spirit is overcome and my heart is full of fear. (Psalm 143:4)

Put all your troubles on him, for he takes care of you. (1 Peter 5:7)

Be merciful to me, O God, be merciful to me. For my soul trusts in you.
And I will hope in the shadow of your wings, until iniquity passes away.
(Psalm 57:1)

The Lord is near the broken-hearted, he is the savior of those whose spirits are crushed down. (Psalm 34:18)

_____

_____

_____

_____

_____

_____

_____

_____

_____

_____

_____

_____

_____

_____

_____

_____

_____

_____

_____

Blessed are those who mourn, for they will be comforted. (Matthew 5:4)

And he said unto them, Why are ye fearful, O ye of little faith?
(Romans 8:26)

Come to me, all you who are troubled and weighted down with care,
and I will give you rest. (Matthew 11:28)

Let my prayer come to your ears, O Lord, and give attention to my cry, make an answer to my weeping... (Psalm 39:12)

He makes the broken-hearted well, and puts oil on their wounds.
(Psalm 147:3)

Do not give me up, O Lord, O my God, be near to me. Come quickly to give me help, O Lord, my salvation. (Psalm 38:21-22)

In the time of my fear, I will have faith in you. (Psalm 56:3)

God, my rock, in him will I take refuge... (2 Samuel 22:2-3)

The God of all grace who has given you a part in his eternal glory through Christ Jesus, will himself give you strength and support, and make you complete in every good thing. (1 Peter 5:10)

I was crying to God with my voice, even to God with my voice, and he gave ear to me. (Psalm 77:1)

Then let us come near to the seat of grace without fear, so that mercy may be given to us, and we may get grace for our help in time of need. (Hebrews 4:16)

Now may the God of hope make you full ... through faith, so that all hope may be yours in the power of the Holy Spirit. (Romans 15:13)

Deliver me out of the mire, and let me not sink ... (Psalm 69:14)

... For you are my lamp, O Lord, and the Lord will make the dark
bright for me. (2 Samuel 22:29)

God is our refuge and strength, a very present help in trouble.
(Psalm 46:1)

_____

_____

_____

_____

_____

_____

_____

_____

_____

_____

_____

_____

_____

_____

_____

_____

_____

_____

_____

_____

_____

_____

_____

Put your cares on the Lord, and he will be your support... (Psalm 55:22)

Trust in the Lord with all thine heart, and lean not unto thine own understanding. (Proverbs 3:5)

Be my strong Rock, the strong place of my salvation, for you are my
Rock, and my safe place. (Psalm 71:3)

Put your life in the hands of the Lord, have faith in him... (Psalm 37:5)

And the peace of God, which is deeper than all knowledge, will keep your hearts and minds in Christ Jesus. (Philippians 4:7)

But the Lord is the savior of the upright, he is their strength in the time of trouble. (Psalm 37:39)

And our hope for you is certain, in the knowledge that as you take part in the troubles, so you will take part in the comfort. (2 Corinthians 1:7)

Be on the watch, unmoved in the faith, and be strong...
(1 Corinthians 16:13)

Take your rest in the Lord, waiting quietly for him ...... (Psalm 37:7)

Before the sun is up, my cry for help comes to your ear, my hope is in your words. (Psalm 119:147)

_____

_____

_____

_____

_____

_____

_____

_____

_____

_____

_____

_____

_____

_____

_____

_____

_____

_____

_____

Have faith in him at all times, let your hearts go flowing out before him.
God is our safe place. (Psalm 62:8)

Let the story of your mercy come to me in the morning, for my hope is in you. Give me knowledge of the way in which I am to go, for my soul is lifted up to you. (Psalm 143:8)

I will keep God in memory, with sounds of grief, my thoughts are troubled, and my spirit is overcome. (Psalm 77:3)

_____

_____

_____

_____

_____

_____

_____

_____

_____

_____

_____

_____

_____

_____

_____

_____

_____

In my trouble my voice went up to the Lord, and my cry to my God ...
and my prayer came to his ears. (2 Samuel 22:7)

...Take heart and be strong, have no fear and do not be troubled, for
the Lord your God is with you wherever you go. (Joshua 1:9)

...Keep where you are and have no fear, now you will see the salvation
of the Lord which he will give you today... (Exodus 14:13)

But those who are waiting for the Lord will have new strength, they will get wings like eagles, running, they will not be tired, and walking, they will have no weariness. (Isaiah 40:31)

... And the light goes on shining in the dark,
it is not overcome by the dark. (John 1:5)

_____

_____

_____

_____

_____

_____

_____

_____

_____

_____

_____

_____

_____

_____

_____

_____

_____

_____

_____

But my eyes are turned to you, O Lord God, my hope is in you...
(Psalm 141:8)

... I was full of trouble and sorrow. Then I made my prayer to the Lord, saying, O Lord, take my soul out of trouble. (Psalm 116:3-4)

Be strong ... for your work will be rewarded. (2 Chronicles 15:7)

... for the things which are seen are for a time,
but the things which are not seen are eternal. (2 Corinthians 4:18)

That I may have knowledge of him, and of the power of his coming
back from the dead, and a part with him in his pains,
becoming like him in his death. (Philippians 3:10)

And now, Lord, what am I waiting for? My hope is in you. (Psalm 39:7)

I am able to do all things through him who gives me strength.
(Philippians 4:13)

God is with me as a mighty one... (Jeremiah 20:11)

As for me, here I am in your hands, do with me whatever seems good and right in your opinion. (Jeremiah 26:14)

So you have sorrow now, but I will see you again,
and your hearts will be glad, and no one will take away
your joy. (John 16:22)

... Have in mind the orders through the Lord Jesus. For the purpose of God for you is this: that you may be holy ... (1 Thessalonians 4:3)